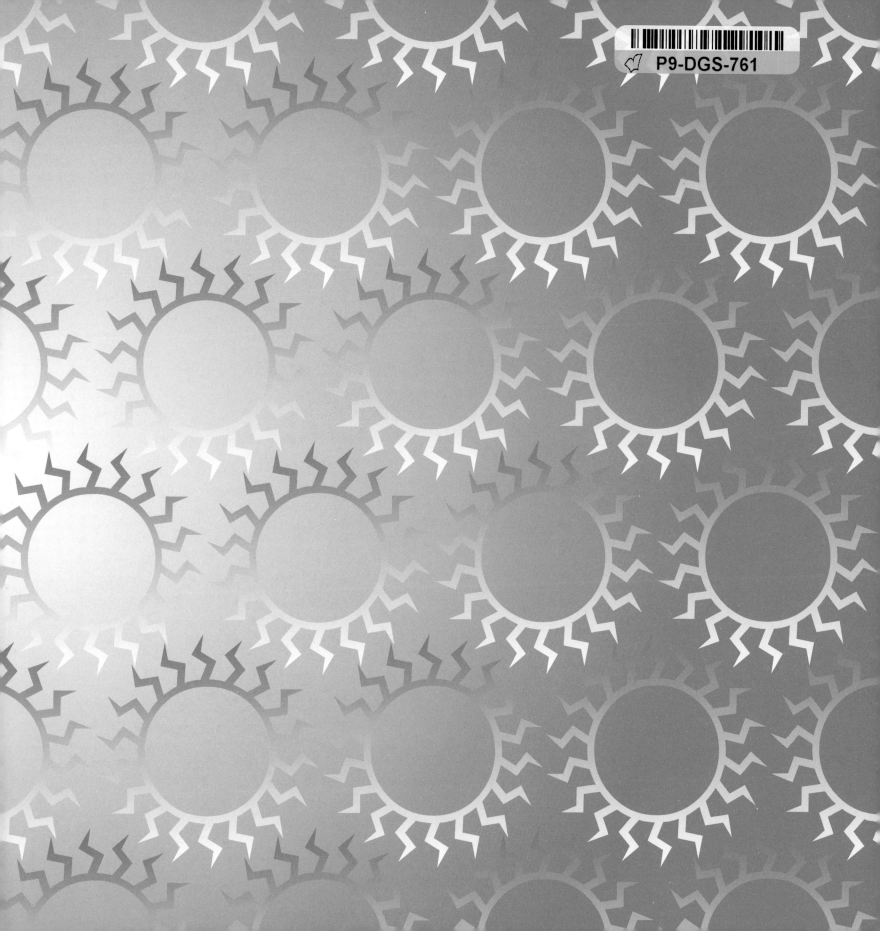

# THE *New* Southwest Home

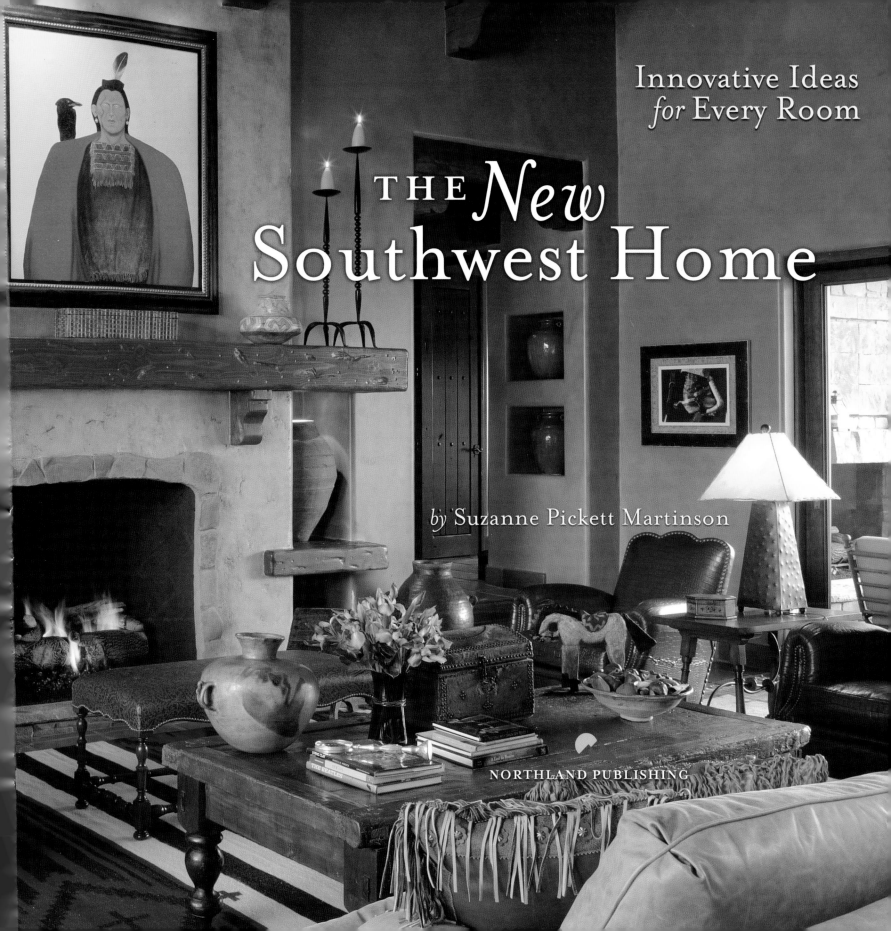

Innovative Ideas
*for* Every Room

# THE *New* Southwest Home

*by* Suzanne Pickett Martinson

NORTHLAND PUBLISHING

For the beautiful cover image, we would like to extend a special thank you to photographer Jeff Green and Phoenix Home & Garden editor Linda J. Barkman and art director/photo stylist Margie Van Zee.

www.northlandbooks.com

Composed in the United States of America
Printed in China

Edited by Tammy Gales
Designed by David Jenney
Production supervised by Donna Boyd

FIRST IMPRESSION 2004
ISBN 10: 0-87358-857-6
ISBN 13: 978-0-87358-857-7

08  07  06    5  4  3  2

Library of Congress Cataloging-in-Publication Data

Martinson, Suzanne Pickett. The Southwest Home : innovative ideas for every room / Suzanne Pickett Martinson.
    p.  cm.
            1. Interior decoration—Southwest, New.  I Title.

NK2002.M375 2004         747'.0979—dc22
            2004053167

# { contents }

1   *introduction*

3   *first impressions*
## Entryways

13   *gathering together*
## Family & Living Rooms

33   *heart of the home*
## Kitchens

49   *private retreats*
## Sleeping Rooms

71   *bathing beauties*
## Bathrooms

89   *special occasions*
## Wine, Dine, & High-Tech

117   *body & soul*
## Rejuvenate

127   *creating a balanced home*
## Work & Play

135   *acknowledgements*

136   *resources*

The use of warm colors and varied textures in this living space evokes the feelings of comfort and peace. Stone flooring and boulders built into the walls provide an earthy foundation for the rich tones of the furniture and southwestern accessories. Architectural elements, such as the circular ceiling pattern in the dining room and the cozy seating arrangement in the living room, create a natural sense of separation for the rooms yet allow the general spaces to remain open and fresh.

# { introduction }

HOME. This simple word stands for so much, yet it can be as basic or elaborate as you wish. And since Southwest style embraces a wide variety of influences, chances are you will be drawn to what feels right. The concept of home really isn't about how small or large your home's physical space is, but instead it revolves around the emotions that are generated from and within your personal space—feelings like safety and security, pleasure and passion, strength and serenity. It is a place of refuge, renewal, and escape.

In the Southwest, sunlight plays a dominant role in the art of architecture and design. Structural elements such as deep porches and window overhangs help buffer the strong sun, while expansive windows and sliding glass doors welcome light into all corners of the home. Using those and other common elements, a blend of styles that make up the Southwest have emerged, offering the opportunity to create a home that combines a myriad of styles that reflect your personal taste.

So, if you are looking for that place to call home, try connecting with your heart to discover what it needs to feel centered. Perhaps you long for a peaceful bedroom painted in your favorite color or a bright and lively kitchen space to share with family and friends. A hidden reading nook or meditation space might be your desire, or even a self-indulgent bathroom with pampering amenities like a sauna and steam shower. Your special place could be found in any southwestern style—from traditional territorial ranch to Southwest contemporary.

Creating a home that appeals to you is one of life's significant challenges. Make it a priority to uncover your needs, identify your desires, and experience the joy of making your house a home. So what are you feeling right now? Does something stand out? Your answer may be a clue to where your journey begins. To help spark your imagination, this book offers creative ideas and visual examples of how others have achieved their home design goals. Illustrated by a fusion of design and architectural influences, these images represent the ever-evolving diversity of styles that make up today's Southwest home.

# Entryways

*Right:* The entryway of this southwestern-themed home is a delight. The gentle curving architectural patterns are awash in a textured subtle yellow that acts as the perfect backdrop for the colorful Indian art, textiles, and accessories. Neutral tones of the flagstone flooring and the coffee-colored custom front door are joined by oversized pots and an overhead light in matching colors.

*Opposite:* When entering this home, you can see straight to the other side of the house. The narrow passageway serves to pique the interest of guests, particularly with the art found along the way. Windows installed at the top of the wall encourage light to pass through.

# { *first impressions* }

IT IS WELL KNOWN that it only takes five seconds to make a first impression. This is true for people, places, and even your home. And while it is important to make sure your home offers a good impression to others, it is even more important that you, the homeowner, feel good about your home's environment. After all, you are the one living there day in and day out.

One of the first things encountered when entering a residence is the entryway. Sometimes called a foyer, entrance hall, reception area, or vestibule, this typically cozy space greets your guests, welcomes friends, and acts as a transition between the outer world and your inner life.

Entryways can also set the tone for the rest of the home's décor. Contemporary or country, Santa Fe or Mediterranean, your home's entrance provides a glimpse into the design personality of your abode, kind of like a sneak peak into a box full of treasures. An oversized mirror, an antique coat stand, a distressed side table, or a striking piece of art can be a dramatic yet hospitable accent that instantly intrigues the mind, making you wonder what lies around the next corner.

In the Southwest, natural sunlight is often used as part of the home's entry. Whether through skylights, clerestory windows, stained glass side door panels, or clear glass incorporated into the front door, the southwestern sun can play an important part of the entry's color, design, and mood. Integrating natural light with personal items, such as an artistic tray of champagne flutes or a functional mail catch or key holder, can greatly enhance the warmth of your home's entryway, giving all who enter a wonderful first impression.

The interior entryway is a transitional space between the world outside the home and the dimensions of life of the occupants inside. According to the nature and personality of the family, the impression of the interior entryway may project an ambiance of traditional values, intimacy, grandeur, or historic sensibilities. If designed successfully, the interior entryway prepares the visitor or guest for the life and attitudes within the home itself.

—CHARLES SCHIFFNER
Architect, Schiffner & Associates

Top left: The arched entry wall takes the shape of the home's architecture and frames the curve of the front door beyond. Inside the courtyard, there's enough space for a fountain, pots of flowers, and even a table with chairs. Pay attention to the exterior entry as well as the interior—one blends into the other, and if carefully planned, it can create quite an impression. Bottom left: The use of lights is important when setting the stage for your home's entry. Although it is best to avoid harsh, glaring lights, it is a good idea to have some lights that are bright enough to see clearly when needed, and softer accent and spot lighting for special effects. Opposite: Outside entries can set the tone for the interior passageway. Here, stone flooring used outside is carried through to the inside of the home. Oversized boulders, native landscaping, a soothing pond, and a blazing fire create a feeling of welcome anticipation.

When entering this home, there is no doubt that the homeowners love the Old West. The use of stone floors and wooden architectural elements, combined with the furnishings, carry out the theme. Accessories like the saddle, lariat, canteen, and cowboy boots arranged in the entry niche, the rifle standing guard at the door, and the branding iron chandelier are authentic to the way of life in the Old West and bring back fond memories of favorite cowboy shows.

*Above:* **It's a feast for the eyes when entering this home! Greeted by an Indian headdress and a canoe suspended from the ceiling, guests can't help but stop and gaze in wonderment. Floor to ceiling stone pillars frame the stairs that lead to the second level. Clerestory windows welcome light into the space and act as a border for the high walls.** *Top right:* **A shallow entryway doesn't have to be boring. In this space, visitors are greeted by an antique table holding southwestern artifacts, and they are then taken on a journey down the hallway with original artwork every step of the way. Establish a focal point for your entry, as with the table here, to bring the focus inside and set the tone for the rest of the home.** *Bottom right:* **The custom entry door on the right is bordered by a wall of rough stone and opens to a roomy vestibule. Iron candelabras and a painting reside on one side and a collection of Kachina dolls and baskets on the other. A large iron chandelier is suspended from the towering ceiling bringing attention upwards.**

*Entryways often get overlooked when it comes to design. To create interest and per-sonality to these somewhat small yet visible spaces, try adding unique wall sconces and a warm, textured Venetian finish on the walls. Or, use a pedestal to hold a vase of your favorite flowers, or an entry table to display cherished heirloom objects.*

—JEFF ZISCHKE, *Artist & Designer, Zischke Studios*

*Opposite:* The golden hued faux-finished walls in this entry provide an appealing backdrop for artwork and rustic acces-sories. The multi-colored slate flooring picks up the tone of the walls, ironwork, and wooden door and beams. When needed for large gatherings, there is enough space to add a greeting table or hold a receiving line.
*Right:* Stacked stone covers the entry walls to this home, creating a seamless transition from the exterior to the interior. Polished stone floors pick up the colors of the rough stone and the floor's dark border leads guests into the main areas of the home. Lighting and decorative accents in iron coordinate with the front door and other wood furnishings throughout the home.

Against a white background, the contemporary furnishings in this angled entryway are prominently showcased. The large mirror and side table anchor the space. A custom cabinet holds a collection of colored glass bottles and the patterned rug leads the way to the rest of the home.

*Left:* The use of color and design work in tandem to create magnificent art-work out of the functional stairs. A blue cylinder holds a red orb, standing out against the brilliant yellow. It may be hard to move visitors away from this stunning entry space.

*Right:* The beauty of this door is best seen as it opens on the diagonal. The wooden door, like a moving sculpture, promises more surprises inside!

*Opposite:* The entry to this home is through the gallery-like path leading to other areas of the home. The white walls and dark flooring ground the oversized art collection, while spot lighting focuses on individual paintings. A sculpture, positioned in the corner, greets passersby.

# Family & Living Rooms

Right: The clean contemporary lines and the tan and olive color scheme produce a cool, serene setting in this living room. A two-tiered glass coffee table is the center of a variety of seating choices. The custom cabinetry has a place for everything from favorite sculptures to a hidden television. Opposite: Pillows can be removed from the built-in seating to open the hidden closets behind. A chaise, for sitting or napping, is positioned close to the fireplace. With base colors of cream and brown dictating the living room design, the more colorful painting seems to effortlessly draw attention.

# { gathering together }

THERE'S SOMETHING TO BE SAID about a comfy, inviting room. In fact, if your family room or living room isn't comfortable, chances are it will never be used, defeating the purpose of having a designated space where your family can relax and spend time together, or where you can easily entertain others.

In recent years, the concept of the Southwest family room has expanded to oftentimes include an entertainment system, computer workspace, game tables, play areas, and adjacent access to the kitchen. Also called a great room, these multi-functional family rooms serve as the gathering place for a multitude of daily activities.

Living rooms, whether formal or casual, also function as a destination within your home where people are encouraged to sit down, relax, and communicate with one another. For many, though, living rooms are often underused and sometimes even abandoned in favor of the more relaxed family room atmosphere. If your living room isn't one of your top room choices when it comes to entertaining guests, it might be time to find out how to make it more appealing.

One simple way to enhance the atmosphere in your living room or family room is to design the sitting areas so conversation can easily flow. Likewise, your choice of furniture affects the amount of time spent in the room. And wisely chosen paint colors, fabric textures, and flooring will add to the overall comfort of the environment.

Finally, when arranging furniture or choosing window treatments, don't forget to take the beauty of the southwestern views into consideration. Many people would pay a premium to be able to see the daily, ever-changing colors of an early morning sunrise or late afternoon sunset.

Above: Full of textures—a stacked stone fireplace, chenille couches, a wool rug, and a leather ottoman—this corner room with a view is stunning. With butt-glazed windows extending at an angle, the native landscape and surrounding mountains are in full view. An unobtrusive large screen television is positioned in the recessed wall and storage is tucked away in custom cabinetry below. Left: Framing a spectacular view, this large picture window is the focal point of the family's gathering spot. Ample seating that encourages relaxation surrounds a stacked stone fireplace. The subtle lighting gives the room a cozy glow.

*Living in the Southwest, our architecture tends to include large windows—inviting the bright sun to come in. My best advice is to have no fear of strong color. Soft, safe shades will only wash out in our strong bright light. Try using all shades of red, straw gold, and cocoa brown in a myriad of textures.*

— JANA PARKER LEE
*Partner & Senior Designer, Wiseman and Gale Interiors*

*Top left: Native boulders are used as a portion of a wall in the interior of this home, creating a natural progression to the mountains outside. The colors of the room are of the earth and with the built-in seating and landscape painting, the room is transformed into a part of the external environment. Above: Family space doesn't have to be a big space. But it does have to have certain elements to make it functional. When purchasing furniture, it is important to make sure that it is comfortable for extended periods of time. Otherwise, chances are you and your family won't use it very often. Here, a couch and lounge chair offer hours of pleasure for watching the fire, enjoying conversation, or reading your favorite novel. Bottom left: This room is all about the view! The series of upper windows and lower doors allow all-encompassing views of the landscape, mountains, and sky. Ceiling fans are placed above the windows to help airflow in the spacious room. Even with a piano and furnishings, there is plenty of room to entertain, especially when the furniture is moved to make way for large gatherings or dancing.*

*Top:* Working with a large space allows you the opportunity to create a variety of distinct areas within one room. In this family room, there are several groupings of comfortable furniture that work well for an intimate chat for two or a party of twelve. One large area rug connects the various arrangements and the color choice of browns and creams is consistent throughout the room.

*Bottom:* If you are fortunate enough to have a basement, just think of the possibilities! The entire basement of this home hosts a multi-functional family room. With a fully equipped kitchen and bar, bistro seating, big screen television, and plump couches, it is no wonder that it is a favorite gathering spot in the home. To prevent a feeling of claustrophobia from being underground, a generous amount of light was used—spot lighting on the ceiling, sconces on the beams, hanging lights and under-the-counter lighting in the kitchen, and freestanding lamps. Additionally, the light-colored stairwell walls are lit and the flooring is in a light tan, keeping it all light and airy.

*Less is more. Using larger pieces of furniture is preferable, and fewer of them, so everything looks less cluttered. Larger-scaled furniture makes more of a statement and also tends to make a room look larger.*
—SUZANNE SMITH
*Allied ASID,*
*Suzanne Smith Interiors*

Natural materials like the stacked stone used for the fireplace and the wooden beams used to create the inlaid ceiling pattern help center this spacious living room. With the pleasing colors of the furnishings and faux-finished walls, the room feels comfortable and cozy. Extra seating is available on either side of the fireplace.

An oversized hand-carved stone fireplace is the center of attention in this family room. On the upper portion, trompe l'oeil leaves fall gracefully around the bust resting on the mantel. Below, the large custom iron grill offers a close-up view of magnificent nighttime fires.

Family rooms are quintessential American spaces, and today's floor plans are strongly dictated by lifestyle. For the most part, people still look to the family room as the primary gathering point in the home. A close proximity to the kitchen facilitates interaction and ease of food and beverage consumption. And fireplaces, media centers, large comfortable furnishings, and bars are all part of the typical thought behind the multi-functionally designed family room.

—ERIC LINTHICUM, *President, Linthicum Custom Builders*

*Above:* **The curving shape of this fireplace expands into two adjoining rooms. On one side, two chairs and an ottoman beckon, while a daybed on the other invites a quick nap. Following the half circle, additional seating flows toward the series of illuminated French doors.** *Top right:* **Red, beige, and green are the predominant colors of this living room and are repeated in the furnishings, accessories, window treatments, and flooring. The result is a serene and classic setting. The stone fireplace mantel is wide enough to hold large accessories that complement the heavy decorative mirror above.** *Bottom right:* **What could be more appealing than a family room created exclusively for enjoyment? Whether you are snuggling on the couch watching the fire glow or watching the sky evolve outside, the room's massive stone fireplace and wood beams above establish a solid foundation.**

Left: Although overhead lighting and candles provide enough light for this family gathering spot, it is the chandelier that draws most of the attention and separates the space from the other adjacent rooms. With an open floor plan and barn-like architecture, creating distinct areas can be achieved with significant elements like a light fixture, painting, or an area rug.

Above: The comfortable Southwest design of this family room is enhanced by the use of varied lighting options. Staying away from overhead lights because of the ceiling beams, the homeowners opted to use a decorative chandelier, wall lighting, and freestanding lamps.

Taking advantage of the southwestern sun, French doors that open to an extended open-slatted porch and clerestory windows are used in succession across the expanse of this living room. A trio of chandeliers, freestanding lights, and candles romantically continue the job at nightfall.

The flower-inspired chandelier is a showstopper in this spacious living area. Similar patterned wall sconces surround the perimeter. Back-to-back couches create natural separate seating areas with a stone fireplace on one side and a baby grand piano on the other. The wood flooring, posts, and beams create a border for the arched picture window and side panels and add a rustic twist to the design.

21

*Top:* The large contemporary painting is the heart of this room. The underlying colors of the living space are derived from the artwork with dashes of accent colors thrown in. The furnishings and floor pattern are placed at an angle and with the painting, form an interesting perspective. A sculpture on the floor appears to be crawling to meet the subject in the painting.

*Bottom:* Ahhh—the look of an uncluttered room. Although your design style doesn't need to be modern to be uncluttered, take a look around and see what doesn't need to be in your space. If you have spectacular views or a stunning piece of art, the goal should be to focus on what makes the room special. Here, the dazzling views of the horizon are enhanced by the contemporary design. With so many light control options available, consider installing a dimmer timer or photoelectric cell so that lighting in the room can automatically match the setting sun.

Collections are most effective when displayed in a group together. Good lighting will greatly enhance the impact of your collection. And by painting the wall behind your collection a lighter or darker color, you will create a more dramatic effect.

—MARIEANN GREEN SEEGER
ASID, IIDA, *Marieann Green Interior Design*

*Top:* The sophisticated look of black doesn't mean that it has to be formal. Here, leather couches you can sink in to are accessorized with plump pillows. A colorful painting sits over the couch and a bowl of bright lemons perk up the coffee table. The stone floors and area rug are neutral in tone, providing a calm foundation for the room.

*Middle:* The upper balcony is a family favorite. With amenities like a fireplace and unlimited views, the sunken room is carpeted and furnishings are upholstered in fabrics that are easy to maintain. The room has color and personality without clutter.

*Bottom:* A visual delight, this family room's architectural elements are works of art. The interesting gas pipes connecting the fireplace to the ceiling are like sculptures, and the varied windows are like paintings of the outdoors. Several seating areas and a dining table offer their different points of view.

*There is beauty in the simplicity and refined lines of this living room space. From the furnishings—the black leather and steel couches and the square glass coffee table—to the materials like the concrete floor and partial room dividers, the design is clean and refreshing. To complete the picture, expansive full-length glass doors provide an unobstructed view of the outdoors.*

*Opposite: The beehive fireplace is the focal point for this cozy nook. The colors of red, yellow, and purple used in the fireplace design are carried through to the rug and other accents. Wood beams, posts, and doors complement the neutral colors of the walls and flooring. With two overstuffed chairs and an ottoman, this is the ideal space to relax with a morning cup of coffee or catch up with your spouse at the end of the day. Top: A collection of Indian rugs and other signature art pieces are showcased in this earth-toned setting, allowing them to be easily seen and appreciated. Dark wood elements such as the entry door, built-in entertainment cabinet, ceiling beams, and tables balance the room's light-colored walls and fabrics. Bottom: Found throughout this multipurpose living space, splashy accents of red are lively and fun. The design on the cabinets is picked up on the upholstered chairs in front of the fireplace. Similar patterned cushions were added to the dining chairs, and the Indian rugs scattered about pull the spaces together.*

Tucked close to the fireplace amidst Southwest-style paintings, pillows, and rugs, two slip-covered chairs in white serve as the daily meeting spot for the homeowners. With a kick-your-feet-up table and shutters to control the light, this snug area is an example of how to create a special place in a small space.

*Far left:* Ideal for a glass of wine or a casual game of chess, a multi-functional table rests between two overstuffed chairs. The room is designed with the calming colors of brown and taupe, creating a romantic ambiance. The corner arrangement makes good use of space and becomes a focal point for the room. *Left:* Surrounded by candles, a glowing fire, and a high-tech CD system, this duo of chairs offers much needed pampering. The rich walls, plants, and area rug envelope the arrangement and create a space conducive to music appreciation. If you are looking to design an intimate space, step back and take a look around. With a little imagination and some furniture rearranging, you might already have the perfect spot right in front of you.

*Opposite:* Bringing the elements of nature inside, this room is designed to be thoroughly enjoyed. The couch is upholstered in a flower-patterned chenille, while the chair and ottoman are as vibrant as red geraniums. Dried flower arrangements and a still life adorn the mantel. The potted tree, sculptural in its appearance, transitions the eye to the outside views. The neutral tone of the walls and earthy fireplace enable nature to be appreciated.

The curves, angles, and textures of this family room make it engaging and fun! Echoed in the leather furniture, the patterns can be seen throughout the room in the copper sculpture, wavy lighting fixture, and iron fireplace surround. The original artwork cascading down the fireplace wall also uses various elements of shape and color that continue to intrigue. It's hard to stop smiling in this room.

*Top:* The linear pattern found on the ceiling that also frames the fireplace and entertainment system is repeated in the lines of the drapery. The wall pattern also functions as a visual divider between adjoining rooms. Soft colors and contemporary furniture result in a cool, comfortable space. *Bottom:* The sculpture collection stands out in this room of rich browns. Standing on a table and displayed in built-in cabinetry, the art seems to come alive among the furnishings. This is a space for gathering with friends and family or for snuggling up with your most cherished book.

*Above:* The use of wood ceiling beams in this living room is carried throughout the home and is used as a room divider as well. Similar in color, the coffee table, bar cabinets, and kitchen cabinetry complete the theme. A patterned sectional can accommodate a crowd and the open floor plan is ideal for entertaining. *Top right:* As interesting as any design element in the room, this ceiling employs a variety of different artistic techniques. Square blocks of Saltillo tile are spaced in a grid-like pattern on the ceiling and the angled heads of beams ring the perimeter where the wall and ceiling meet. A border of colorful tile rests under the beam heads. The accompanying furnishings pull colors from the ceiling. The walls, painted an off-white, hold the design together. *Bottom right:* The multi-layer ceiling design forms a dramatic frame for the golf course close at hand and the mountain peak view in the distance. The layered effect is carried through to the fireplace and window treatments. Using the mountain as a guide, off-white and beige are the primary colors. The effect is cool and tranquil.

*Dark wooden beams outline the structure of this home's pitched ceiling against the toffee-colored faux walls. Wood, used on both the ceiling and the floor, is carried throughout the architectural elements and the furnishings. Unexpectedly, the furniture is positioned at an angle, giving it a new point of view. Stone flooring and a lower ceiling in the kitchen further separate the two rooms. With a sliding glass panel that opens to the back patio the inside and outside mingle as one.*

31

# Kitchens

*Right:* The clean lines of this contemporary kitchen are emphasized by the wood cabinetry and flooring and the use of black and steel. An oversized center island, with a second sink specifically for prep work, makes cooking and serving a pleasure. Underneath are two dishwashers, a must for those who entertain large groups frequently. *Opposite:* Elegant and comfortable, the dining area is close enough to the kitchen to chat with the cook yet far enough removed to maintain privacy if needed. Stone flooring helps to visually separate the two areas. When not in use, the glass dining table is a perfect spot to feature a large blooming plant or favorite sculpture.

# { *heart of the home* }

KITCHENS ARE LIKE MAGNETS. Families hang out there—reading, doing homework, eating, and catching up on the day's events. Guests tend to drift there, standing around and sipping wine while you cook. Even in large parties, you'll find pockets of people camped out in the kitchen's various nooks and crannies. So what gives?

The lure of the kitchen revolves around food, of course—the smells, the sights, the anticipation of the tastes. The process of food preparation, then, is a big draw, but the atmosphere of the kitchen is also determined by the care and attention to details that make it welcoming and user-friendly.

Details such as the smooth texture of a granite countertop, the rough-hewn surface of the floor and matching backsplash, or the warm glow from an incandescent hanging light can spark a feeling of comfort. Or it could be that the gleam of stainless steel appliances or the comfort of country French cabinets appeal to your senses and set your body at ease. The food warmer, under counter ice machine, or built-in steam oven might be exactly what you need to entertain more efficiently. Whatever your pleasure, you can be sure that others will sense your appreciation and respond favorably as well.

Most kitchens in the Southwest also have the added benefit of hosting multiple windows that offer natural light and visual interest. Sometimes skylights are installed for more effect, and many kitchens open up onto family rooms or great rooms, further creating a spacious and roomy ambiance. Sunny, soothing, quiet, or energetic, choosing your preferred colors can further transform the room and evoke a familiar sense of hearth and home.

And finally, a kitchen's layout is crucial to efficient and pleasurable food preparation while enhancing the comfort of those simply hanging out. American writer and humorist E.B. White said it best. "On days when warmth is the most important need of the human heart, the kitchen is the place you can find it."

*Opposite: In the European style, this kitchen is glowing with the warmth of wood and efficiency of steel. The center island is multifunctional with a prep sink and warming drawers below and a raised dining bar on the opposite side. Two built-in ovens are the only other obvious appliances. All others are hidden behind the cabinetry. A table and chairs close at hand provide in-kitchen dining for family meals or entertaining. Top right: This kitchen has it all. The center island features a granite prep area behind the eating bar, and the half-moon counter—underneath a dramatic steel circle—serves as a buffet. Muted glass doors on the cabinets give a hint of the items inside. A large window welcomes plenty of sunlight, complementing the kitchen wall color and cabinetry. Bottom: With enough space to cook and host guests, this kitchen is a model of efficiency. The hood, descending majestically from the ceiling, sheds light on the tasks at hand. Additional lighting is attached to the metal square also originating from the ceiling. Kitchen stools make it easy to grab a quick bite or to sit and chat as food is prepared.*

*People now acknowledge that most gatherings happen in the kitchen and that space needs to accommodate entertaining as well as the function of meal preparation. So, seating for socializing around the prep area is a consideration as is built-in or freestanding casual dining. Answering questions as to how you live and entertain will help identify your optimum design.*

—MIKE HIGGINS
*Architect, Higgins Architects*

A concrete island and parallel countertop create quite an impression. Since there are no cabinets, kitchen tools and accessories are attached to the wall or placed in open shelves over and under the countertops. A freestanding baker's rack holds wine glasses and the homeowners' collection of masks and jugs sits on a shelf near the ceiling. Concrete floors extend to the dining area. With a large doorway that offers views to the outside, the kitchen can easily acquire privacy behind closed doors if desired.

*Left:* The use of wood on the cabinets is matched in the flooring to give this kitchen a feeling of space. Floor borders of a different material outline the center island and the perimeter of the cabinetry. A series of windows allows light to be an integral part of the interior design and offers views to the desert landscape outside. *Below:* Industrial rubber surfacing is used for the flooring in this modern kitchen. Yellow and black cabinetry is a fresh approach. Stainless steel appliances and dining table are sophisticated accents. With the mountains right outside, large glass doors and a narrow window near the ceiling bring in light and nature.

*Top: The functional spaces of this great room radiate from the kitchen. The open, roomy structure of the space allows an easy flow from one area to the other. The kitchen's rectangular island provides room for prepping and eating at the bar. A dining table is nearby, as is casual seating for four and a cozy arrangement around the fireplace. Windows placed on high keep the space bright and cheery.*
*Bottom: This country kitchen is full of charm. With ample counter space surrounding the island, there is room for multiple projects or multiple cooks! An overhead pot rack that matches the cabinetry holds copper cookware and baskets of dried herbs, while a rooster claims his territory on top. Wallpaper is used to bring flowers into the space and decorative stained glass windows are placed above the upper cabinets. Cookbooks are housed under the kitchen island within easy reach.*

The kitchen will always be the heart of the home, so function and style need to be addressed. For example, functional elements such as islands and pantries provide more warmth and interest when created to look like furniture. Also, using drawers for the lower kitchen cabinets is much easier and functional for the cook and for the person cleaning up.

—BESS J. JONES
*Allied ASID, Bess Jones Interiors*

The most important thing to consider when designing a kitchen is the desired experience in that kitchen. What does it feel appropriate for—a gourmet chef, a big family, an entertaining space? Then from that, we layer in functional issues and material selections that make that big vision happen.

—KRISTINE WOOLSEY
Architect, Woolsey Studio

Opposite: The warm colors of this kitchen evoke feelings of hearth and home. Trompe l'oeil painting on the ceiling, the details on the refrigerator/ freezer woodwork, and the candle-like lighting on the pot rack bring design and interest to the upper portions of the kitchen. Ceramic tile, used on the flooring, countertops, and backsplash, continues the sense of texture and substance. And the pattern on the decorative tile that makes up the border on the backsplash is repeated on the pottery hanging above the stove and on the chair fabric.

Top: A pot rack over the center island holds favorite pots and pans within easy reach. Designed with a casual country flair and Old World charm, the kitchen receives glorious sunlight from the arched windows. The kitchen is separated from the dining area beyond with a countertop that steps up to become bar seating on the other side.

Red—on the walls and island cabinetry—is the central color in this well-appointed kitchen. The steel pot rack extends the full length of the island and further enlarges the room. A raised level off the island can be used for dining or as a buffet.

Top left: Drawing attention to the cook's favorite appliance, decorative metal frames the oven and hood. An over-the-stove water faucet makes it a snap to fill pots of water for pasta or steamed veggies. The white cabinetry and stone backsplash are other interesting elements used together to make this kitchen original.

Above: Doesn't this kitchen call to you? The soothing tone of the yellow walls is the backdrop for terra cotta floor tile and a blue center island. A wall mural acts as the backsplash and a pot filler faucet rests to its side.

Left: Custom designed pieces of art made out of metal rest on the tile backsplash and surround the kitchen's elevated fireplace. A filtered water faucet—to ease the awkwardness of filling and moving pots with large amounts of water—is positioned over the stovetop. A rustic candelabra with a trio of red candles and a shallow dish of tomatoes add a spark of rich color.

The layout of this kitchen is well planned and efficient. The stove, across from the sink and center island, features olive-colored textured tiles and a small faucet for filling pots. The rest of the backsplash is neutral in color with accents of green. Easy to reach, plates are stored in open racks above the second sink. Extra storage for kitchen essentials and decorative pots is under the multi-functional island.

This stovetop hood is camouflaged behind the custom wood paneling that complements the kitchen cabinetry. An arched pattern made out of tiles is centered in the backsplash and identifies the range in front. Tucked into the corner, windows provide sunlight during the day and city views at night.

*Opposite:* Inside the stone-stacked arch is a kitchen unto itself. With countertops and cabinetry, stove and hood, the recessed space is a study in detail. A trash compactor and microwave oven are situated under the counters and extra storage is tucked into the corners. The center island opposite is a much sought-after bonus. *Above:* The circular shape of the copper hood is echoed in the semi-circle of the kitchen island and dining bar below. With enough space to seat six comfortably, the dining space allows the cook to enjoy conversation while creating culinary delights for family and guests. *Below:* In this kitchen, the hood over the stovetop is hidden behind the decorative wall treatment that also provides shelf space for favorite accessories and art. Countertops continue around the space and under the windows. The island also offers seating for dining, homework, or games.

*Left:* This kitchen serves as the gathering spot for family and friends, mainly due to the fireplace that bestows the space with warmth and good cheer. A desk in front of the fire is a favorite place to write thank you notes and plan menus. The cabinetry—both built-in and freestanding—is painted a rich blue that is offset by the textured white walls. Terra cotta floor tile, a Native American rug, and southwestern accessories add continuity to the Southwest theme.

*Bottom:* Create something unique out of a weight-bearing post. In this kitchen, a corner fireplace was installed for viewing pleasure from several rooms. Tucked underneath, an arched recess stores firewood. Clean white cabinetry and a patterned backsplash give a cool, serene look to the small space.

*The kitchen is the place where family and friends gather and memories are made. With this in mind, the kitchen's design should be convenient, functional, and equally beautiful.*

—KEVIN DUERMIT

*Vice President, Toll Brothers, Inc.*

*Filled with pattern, texture, and details, this kitchen is anchored by its full-size fireplace. Decorative tile is used on the fireplace ledge and the inside surround that is repeated throughout the kitchen backsplashes. The hand-carved stone mantel lends a sense of sophistication to the space. What a joy to dine on the square table in front of the kitchen fire on a daily basis!*

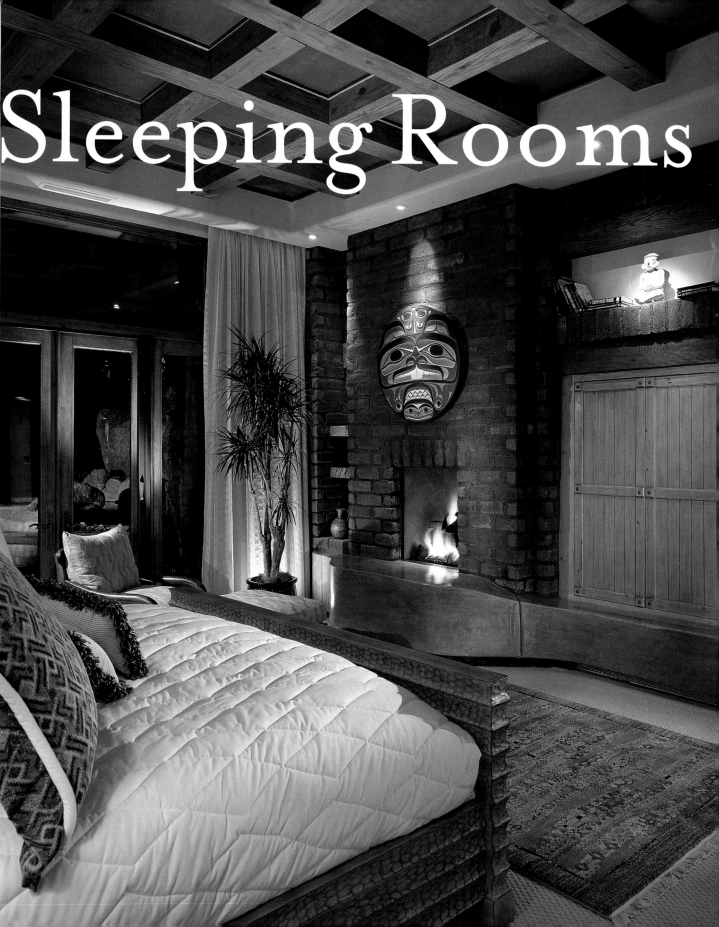

# Sleeping Rooms

*Right:* The warm tones of this bedroom are inviting and peaceful. A lively fire glows in the fireplace set amidst a brick wall, while a spotlight focuses on the round Indian painting above. Wood is a dominant material in the room and is found in the bed frame, doors, shelves, and built-in television cabinet.

*Opposite:* Ebony lions stand guard over the metal-framed bed. Upholstered with fabric that is repeated in the drapery, the colors of black, yellow, red, and white work together in seamless beauty.

# { *private retreats* }

IT IS IMPORTANT for the body's well-being to have peace and quiet on a daily basis. Shutting out the world and cocooning are not just lofty ideals—they are necessary pursuits in today's busy society. Time spent in your bedroom should satisfy those needs for restoration and rejuvenation, replenishing your energy and your spirit.

First and foremost is the body's need for sleep. With medical experts advising that eight hours of sound and restful sleep is essential to maintaining good health, it is obvious that the bedroom's primary focus should be on how to achieve optimum sleep levels. One crucial way to assure a good night's sleep is to make sure you select the right mattress for your back. Another way, highly recommended by sleep experts, is to remove the television from your bedroom, taking away the temptation to fall asleep to the sounds of late night talk shows. Other ways include reducing outside noise levels, installing total light control in the form of window shades and drapery, and increasing good air ventilation.

Certainly the colors you choose to surround you will affect your emotions as well. If your favorite shade is red, use that as your base color or as an accent in your bedspread, lamps, or rugs. If green generates a warm, safe feeling, consider hanging a painting of trees and flowers where you will see it as you awake every morning. And because sunlight is a natural energy source, situating a comfortable reading chair in line with a window that overlooks your native landscape might be just the boost you need to face tomorrow's challenges.

Treating your bedroom like a place of refuge will lead you to de-clutter and refine your space, eliminating all but the basics conducive to a good night's rest. A bedside copy of *Goodnight Moon* wouldn't hurt either.

Do you have a favorite pattern or theme? The use of fabric in the bedroom can make a tremendous difference when striving for a certain effect. Here, floral fabric is used as drapery and bed curtains. Golden tones for other furnishings are pulled from the fabric, and the cool green of the walls and soft coffee-colored tiles balance the patterns. In front of the fireplace, two chairs and a table provide the perfect spot to share a glass of sherry before bed or have morning coffee.

*Extending from large wooden beams, the dramatic draping of velvet is reminiscent of royalty. Coordinating curtains frame desert views outside, and the colors repeat in the floor rug and wall color. Inside the recessed niche is a gold vase with a dried floral arrangement, also an ideal spot for a sculpture or painting. The armoire, similar in color to the bed, hides a television inside.*

**Opposite:** *There is no doubt that a spectacular headboard can make a room stand out. In the case of this ornate wood bed ensemble, it is certainly true. The goal, then, is to add elements that are strong and complement the unique piece without detracting from its glory. Here, the red-rose painting, red and gold overstuffed pillows, and the large gold orbs on the floor do the bed justice.*

**Top:** *A reclaimed rustic gate now serves as a distinctive headboard in this bedroom. Towering ocotillo branches, dried and arranged in an oversized pot, balance the headboard's height near the door to the patio. With off-white walls, carpet, and bedding, the wood elements and painting in this Southwest room are able to take center stage.* **Bottom:** *Set against stone walls, this stair-step wood headboard is a signature piece of furniture. Tones of the dark wood architectural accents and furnishings set the foundation for the room. On a lighter note, a painting sits low to the ground and shares colors with the overstuffed love seat at the end of the bed.*

53

The master bedroom is the most intimate of spaces in the home and should be thought of as a private retreat. Unlike the public spaces of a home, the bedroom needs to satisfy only its occupants. It should be filled with the colors, furnishings, and amenities you love. Be sure to include a few of your very favorite things—a piece of art, a chair you love, a special collection. These will be the last images you see before you turn out the light and the first things you wake to, so they should be meaningful and pleasing to your eye.

—LINDA J. BARKMAN
*Editor, Phoenix Home & Garden*

Wood ceiling beams radiate out from the beehive fireplace, identifying it as a focal point for the bedroom. Situated at an angle, the bed is close enough to the fireplace to get the full effect. Likewise, a chair is placed for maximum enjoyment of the fire and the television hidden behind cabinet doors.

55

*Lighting in the bedroom should be easy on your eyes. Consider floor lamps with up-lighting and table lamps with soft bulbs. If you need light for reading, it should be focused on that particular area only. Swing lamps by the bed are a great solution using either a soft light or a focused light. For a choice of intensity, use a three-way bulb.*

—DENEICE HASE, *Design Director, Robb & Stucky*

*Above:* The antique frame of this incredibly indulgent bed works beautifully with the room's typical Southwest elements like the dark wood ceiling beams and beehive fireplace. Located a step below the sleeping space, a charming seating area features comfy furniture and views of the garden. Partial walls, which further delineate the two spaces, also serve to create a little more privacy for each area so that one person can snooze while the other can read in front of the fire. *Opposite:* Hidden in the sweeping arch over the head of this bed are reading lights that create interesting design patterns on the wall. Tucked into the bed nook are two built-in nightstands that coordinate with the built-in niches and display areas opposite the bed. A television and sound system are neatly hidden in behind the wood doors and a cushy chair and ottoman are a much appreciated addition to the bedroom suite.

*Top: The rich colors of brown and black used in the striped bedding generate a strong sense of design, appealing to the fashion expert of the house. The wood headboard and night table pull strength from the color combination. For a dash of color, red is used for the accent pillows as well as the bench at the foot of the bed. Bottom: Rich colors and textures are used to create a sumptuous feeling to this bedding. In colors of purple and toffee, bedclothes are luxuriously layered. Velvet in deep purple is tied with gold tassels and frames the head of the bed. Window treatments in the same gold and purple sway on top. Opposite: Rustic wooden doors give a hint of the strong design throughout this bedroom. The decorative wood bed and nightstand sit proudly on Mexican tile. Velvet floor cushions and a silk coverlet introduce softer textures, and the use of red and gold textiles skillfully balances the bedroom space.*

*If a bedroom is to function as a retreat from a busy lifestyle, then the essence of a luxurious bedroom comes from the creation of an environment that instills peaceful and restful emotions. This comfort occurs by choosing serene colors (whether light or dark tones) that have grayed undertones as opposed to brighter true colors. Also, the tactile quality of each fabric is extremely important. Soft textures offer extreme comfort like down-filled furniture, pillows, duvets, and feather beds.*

—SHARON ALBER FANNIN

*ASID, Designer, Fannin Interiors*

Opposite: *Dazzling in white, the romantic iron bed sits at an angle and receives dappled sunlight, encouraging an afternoon nap on lazy days. A chandelier sits gracefully overhead. Roses, baby's breath, ivy, and a palm tree indicate the homeowner's love of plants.* Top: *The feeling of cool, white sheets is heaven to the body's senses. A decorative iron headboard sits between a pair of antiqued lamps with matching white lampshades. An heirloom trunk is used for storing extra linens and as a night table. An oversized mirror rests comfortably on the floor, catching the incoming light from the window shutters.* Bottom: *There's something about the color of white when it comes to bedrooms that makes you want to just stretch out and relax. Here, the antique canopy bed is host to a down-filled comforter and pillows in crisp white, a lovely place to lie. From the sliding glass doors, sheer curtains ruffle in the wind. The bedroom, striking because of the white painted brick, is timeless.*

Not like your grandmother's attic, this bedroom in the garret has been transformed. With raw materials like aluminum on the ceilings and natural wood for the beams, the space feels fresh and modern. A Native American rug is a refreshing accent.

The contemporary design of the built-in headboard and side tables also provides display space for special pieces of art or books. The drapery keeps out light when it's time for a quick daytime nap or when you want to linger in the morning. And a freestanding reading lamp and chair await.

*Above:* The bold use of greens and purples in this bedroom is enchanting. With accents of red and black, the colors don't get out of hand but do illicit a feeling of fun and lightheartedness.

*Right:* The dynamic colors and use of shapes in this bedroom are exciting. The wall panels surrounding the fireplace are painted different colors, and lilac carries over the door. The bedspread in red hosts pillows of red and pink, which contrast with the deep blue on the chair. A transparent vase filled with vibrant oranges is placed near the door. Don't be afraid to use color!

In an otherwise neutral room, the varied tones of red, magenta, and purple make a statement on this bed. If you have a favorite color, use it in this way or by painting one or more walls. Splashes of color can also come from a special piece of furniture or cherished piece of artwork.

The brilliant color of red and the sophisticated depth of black make this a stunning room. The space, architecturally geared toward obtaining the best and most impressive views possible, is awe-inspiring.

*A little paint and a lot of creativity make this treehouse-themed child's room a very special place to live. The hand-painted tree on the walls and ceiling appear to shade the play and study area, giving the space a comforting feel. While a ladder leans against the textured tree trunk, stuffed animal friends say hello from their nests. Distressed wood covers the wall with the window view to the trees outside.*

*Right:* In the theme of a quaint country cottage, a Murphy's bed folds down for a good night's sleep. The roof of the cottage was constructed with wood and the painting is trompe l'oeil. A side table is creatively painted to look like a brick post.

*Far right:* With the bed up, there is plenty of space to play! A child's card table and chairs are moved to the center for activities. The underside of the bed is now an integral part of the cottage with a Siamese cat resting on a swinging door.

*Bottom:* What a dream boat! This little boy's bed in the shape of a boat rests on a platform of the same shape. The freestanding bookshelves surround a mural headboard scene of the harbor with a seagull and pelican standing guard. Ships, lighthouses, a life preserver, and fishing rod make this room a sea lover's delight.

*Left:* Fit for a queen, dramatic and colorful bed curtains surround a twin bed furnished with cushy pillows and a reading light. With the large pieces of furniture set against the walls, there is ample space to do homework, play, or daydream. *Opposite:* This refreshing room is done so tastefully that the strong multi-colored shades exist in perfect harmony. From the hand-painted wood pieces like the headboard, trunk, nightstands, and bookshelves to the small decorative paint touches of whimsy on the walls, the effect is happy and energetic. A child's piece of clothing hanging on the door is the only hint that a closet is hidden behind.

To make a child's room really child friendly, it may need to be divided into separate areas—for sleeping, study, play, and maybe even a reading space. If the room is small, a parent may have to think outside the box and begin to visualize the room with different elevations such as lofts and platforms, multi-purpose areas like a window seat for reading with storage below, or a fold-down desk or game table. If considering large or expensive built-ins, remember that as a child grows, they will need less play and more homework/computer space.

—MARILYN JOY-KOLESAR
*Designer, MJK Designs*

# Bathrooms

Right: The multi-colored basin perfectly complements the slate-covered walls and floor and joins the painting in adding a dash of color and artistry. A light under the counter is an interesting design element that works well with the mirror, faucet, and wall sconces.

Opposite: Don't forget to use the walls of your bathroom to showcase your art or collections. The warm color tone in this bathroom and the texture of the tub tile and the metal sculptures provide an earthy feeling. Overhead lighting, flickering candlelight, and natural light from a large window further inspire a feeling of intimacy.

# { *bathing beauties* }

FOR SO LONG, bathrooms were considered an afterthought when it came to design. As long as it had the necessary items— a toilet, sink, and shower—it was considered adequate. Times have changed, though, and bathrooms have become an integral part of the home's design focus.

Essentially an extension of the bedroom, the master bathroom has become more spacious and more thoughtful. Space permitting, placing a comfortable chair and ottoman in the corner of the bathroom can be a welcome respite in between your daily rituals. It can also be the perfect place for a treadmill or exercise bike since it will stare back at you every day, not letting you off the hook. Sound systems—some of them wired into the home's main system—are becoming the norm in most of the newer homes today.

In the Southwest, it isn't unusual to find a glass-enclosed shower with enviable views to the great outdoors, or a Jacuzzi tub next to large glass windows opening onto a lushly planted private courtyard. Mirrors and artwork mingle with telephones and tiny televisions, and laptop computers share space with makeup and toothpaste. People can now manage their lives from the privacy of their own bathrooms.

Children's bathrooms have become more fun and colorful with dozens of options available. Hand-painted designs, wallpaper themes, multi-colored tiles, and a dizzying array of bath accessories make kids' bathrooms a delight for the whole family. Let your child help determine the focus, and they might just spend more time washing their hands and brushing their teeth!

Large or small, bathrooms can represent more than just the basics. Just let your imagination flow like...water.

Bathroom surfaces should be materials that can be easily maintained. Glass, ceramic tiles, and solid surfaces are all good choices, as is natural stone. Concrete can be a great alternative, but like unpolished stone, it needs to be sealed. The style you are trying to achieve will most likely affect the materials you choose, with the most important consideration for a bathroom floor being the slip factor. This basically needs to be achieved by using texture, which can be inherent in the materials such as a honed or tumbled stone, or can be accomplished by using smaller tiles with more grout lines such as mosaics.

—KIM GWOZDZ

*Designer & Owner, Provenance*

*Above:* Old-fashioned claw foot tubs have become popular once again, looking right at home in today's bathroom. With faux-painted walls, decorative tile, a walk-in shower, a plush wool rug, and an original oil painting, the angular space of this room is a true inspiration. If you have a small or odd-shaped space to work with, make sure to take measurements of the room and what you plan to install to ensure a good fit and enough room to move about. *Right:* How wonderful to soak in front of a fireplace! The warm wooden tones of the cabinetry and walls meld with the promised warmth of a fire. An overhead chandelier is an unexpected delight and provides enough light to read your favorite novel. Using unexpected accessories in the bathroom can bring you daily joy.

The freestanding tub is the focal point of this bathroom suite. With patterned marble flooring, formal drapes, trompe l'oeil cabinetry, and gold accessories, the effect is sophisticated and appealing. Just imagine partaking of champagne, caviar, and chocolate as you leisurely soak in hundreds of relaxing bubbles. Ahhh...

Take advantage of the views and fresh mountain air with generous windows and French doors that open to a private patio. Space is used efficiently with built-in cabinetry, recessed shelves, and wide ledges. Natural wood floors and woven baskets connect the bathroom to the great outdoors.

Nestled against glorious boulders, this bathroom features butt-glazed glass panels for a close-up encounter. Soft lighting and neutral colors keep the focus on nature outside. Take a look outside your bathroom window or door and see if there is something—a signature plant, specimen cactus, or flowering tree—that could be visually brought inside.

Have a bath, have a seat! Sunlight streams into this welcoming space for reading, bathing, applying makeup, or just being. Two large windows offer views of the yard and distant mountains, with both shades and curtains available for sun protection and privacy.

*Above:* Make a statement! Placing a prominent border around your powder room may give this otherwise simple room a stylish lift.

*Right:* An ornate frame and wall sconces adorn the faux-finished walls of this powder room. Peeking over the top, a Grecian bust and column look right at home. Glowing candlelight adds a touch of romance. A fresh flower arrangement is also a thoughtful addition.

*This nook is ideal for a uniquely designed off-the-floor basin. The round mirror, circular sink, and overhead lighting give the small space depth and personality.*

*It's only paint! The longing for color, yet fear of color is one of the greatest challenges in the design process. Especially in a bathroom (usually the last of the rooms to be considered) paint can help provide a reflection of yourself as well as create an interesting visual experience. So use color! You'll be happy you did. And besides, if you really don't like it, you can just repaint in another color.*

—MARCIA GRABER, *Designer, Graber Designs*

**Far left:** *Natural light peeks through the sheer curtains and mingles with flickering candles and wall sconces. Lighting on the earth-toned walls and stone floors generates a cozy feeling.*

**Left:** *A crystal chandelier and an antique iron table lamp set the tone for this bathroom. Use a special piece of furniture for towel and accessory storage or to display an heirloom or your child's artwork.*

Above-mounted sinks can be created in a myriad of styles and materials. In this powder room, the rich colors and textures of the stone, faux-finished walls, and accessories are accentuated by the stunning copper basin.

*Far right:* This native-themed bathroom takes its cue from the basin and petroglyph-inspired horse prints. The above-mounted sink gives balance to the large mirror and horizontal counter.
*Right:* A shallow basin follows the Zen tradition of minimalism. Clean, strong, and simple, the effect is soothing.

*Above:* What could be more clean and classic than a glass sink? This beautiful example makes itself right at home in the luxurious surroundings.

*Left:* The heavy wood carved cabinetry and coordinating mirror frame are accentuated by the pale yellow walls, adequate lighting, glowing sink, and iron accessories. The toilet is located on the other side of the stair-step wall. Although small in size, this powder room is striking in its design and use of materials.

The generous use of ranch wood and slate in this bathroom requires strong accessories. Multiple framed mirrors and table lamps give height and dimension to the space. The vanity between the sinks is raised to accommodate a chair comfortably. Natural light from windows above evokes a subterranean ambiance.

*Almost cave-like in appearance, this powder room uses natural tones and textured materials to appeal to the senses. The bottom of the vanity is lit from behind, which makes a bigger impression. The flagstone floor is installed with large expanses of grout in between the pieces to create a very natural look as if randomly placed by nature.*

*When working with a small bathroom, first remove all the visible clutter as it can drown the bathroom. Use recessed shallow cabinets to contain the myriad of toiletries. And, if possible, flood the bathroom with natural light.*

—SARAH SWARTZ WESSEL
*Architect, Tennen Studio*

*Top right:* Glossy brown tiles are used midway on the bathroom walls leaving the upper portion to feature original artwork and a decorative circular mirror. The toilet is neatly hidden on the other side of the wall. *Above right:* The muted glass leg surrounds of the vanity are backlit for an enchanting effect. The hand-crafted frame and other pieces of artwork make this powder room a gallery for unique art. Pale walls and neutral stone floors allow the artwork to bask in the limelight.

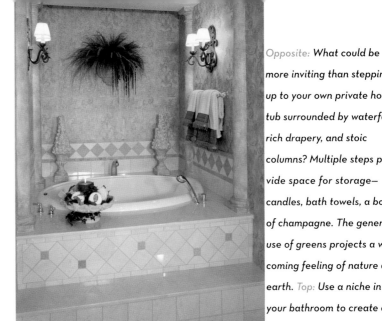

*Opposite:* What could be more inviting than stepping up to your own private hot tub surrounded by waterfalls, rich drapery, and stoic columns? Multiple steps provide space for storage—candles, bath towels, a bottle of champagne. The generous use of greens projects a welcoming feeling of nature and earth. *Top:* Use a niche in your bathroom to create a special bathing area. Consider using at least two steps and an extended platform for easier access into and out of the tub. Have towels within easy reach and add good lighting for those days you need to catch up with the daily newspaper.

*Bottom:* Because bathtubs are narrow, they can be installed in most any size bathroom. By adding several steps, you can also create additional seating space. If you have room, use comfy chairs and side tables to complete the pampering effect. Here, an often used bench features a striped cushion and arm pillows.

Placed on the diagonal, square paper is applied like wallpaper and metal tacks are placed at the points. The walls have a rough texture that works well with the iron hardware, giving the small space a rustic appeal.

*Above:* An under sink light illuminates the basin, and wall sconces throw shadows on the faux-finished walls of this powder room. Simple in design, the effect is dramatic. *Below:* When designing a bathroom, try looking at the possibilities from different perspectives. Here, an original piece of art in the hallway outside the powder room is the inspiration for the bathroom's color scheme. The walls are painted in a soft, muted purple and a spotlight shines on the dried floral arrangement of yellow and bright violet blooms. The circular shape of the mirror frame mimics the round basin, while the rectangle mirror echoes the shape of the door.

The faux finish on the walls pulls in colors from the wood cabinetry, concrete countertop, and framed mirrors. Hidden lighting above and a single focus light center the circular shape of the room. The varied materials used together create an intriguing, but elegant design.

*Opposite:* Wood beams on the ceiling provide continuity from the bedroom to the bathroom, and in this case give a natural feel to the southwestern space. Although the bathroom has no doors, there are clearly defined areas such as the bath, lounge, and dressing room. The home-owners have tastefully chosen to display their Native American art, pottery, and basket collection in this bathroom suite.

*Top:* Unfinished columns mark the entrance to this corner-situated bathtub. They also give balance to the room and its repeated arches, framing the view outside. Pulling the colors together is the dark marble with splashes of white found on the countertops and the bathtub surround. *Bottom:* Instead of typical window treatments, try using a piece of metal art in your bathroom. This piece is open enough to offer a view and let in light, yet it protects enough to feel private.

The bathroom is a perfect room to create a serene personal space. The calming nature of water, natural light, and the scents of soaps and lotions can create a sensuous ambiance and transport us away from our everyday hectic lives. So light some candles, play your favorite music, and close the door. Take advantage of this time to slow down, meditate, and just be.

—CATHERINE ROSS
*Certified Professional Coach,*
*Start Now Coaching*

# Wine, Dine, & High-Tech

*Right: A dynamic piece of art can completely transform a room. Paired with brown leather chairs and a custom dining table, this colorful painting shares honors with a bust perched on a pedestal. With spot lighting above, the custom table also picks up the colors from the painting. Neutral walls allow the color to take center stage.*

*Opposite: It is widely believed that dining tables shaped in a circle promote conversation among guests. In this dining room, not only is the custom wood table round, but the entire room—including the chandelier—is also circular. Resembling a wagon wheel, the ceiling further promotes the motion. Upholstered chairs in a colorful pattern surround the table. The red and brown tones are picked up by the walls, floors, and the artistic doors leading to the kitchen.*

# { *special occasions* }

SPENDING TIME WITH FRIENDS is one of life's treasures. Sharing your home is a gift. So, depending on how—and where—you like to entertain, creating those special areas for others to enjoy is worthy of particular attention.

For many, the formal dining room represents the finest in entertaining. Sometimes the dining room is a separate space—a private enclave. In other homes, the dining room is a primary part of the kitchen and living room sequence. In the southwestern home, the use of light and color tends to dictate the design with many homes taking advantage of expansive windows and French doors, allowing the outside views to create an interesting, inviting environment.

Wine collecting is one of America's fastest growing hobbies, so it is no surprise that the rise in wine storage and wine cellar installations has grown accordingly. From separate rooms equipped with temperature controls and proper storage systems to built-in units and freestanding structures, storing wine in your home is easy and affordable, making impromptu wine tastings and elegant dinners effortless.

Another more recent addition to the home is the media room. Decked out with the latest in technology, media rooms can be part of a family room or den, but oftentimes, they occupy an entirely separate room. With wide screen televisions, powerful sound systems, and a variety of other high-tech options, these rooms are dedicated to the ultimate in entertainment. And comfortable seating can easily be achieved with your favorite style of furniture or with specific chairs designed after those used in commercial movie theaters.

If entertaining others is something that you love, identify those types of situations that bring you the most joy. Whether it be candlelight dinners in the dining room, wine and cheese parties in the cellar, or the latest sci-fi thriller on the big screen, treat yourself to the amenities that help you achieve your goals.

Perfect for a party or an intimate gathering, these tables can be separated to accommodate different activities or put together for a dinner of twelve. Lighting hanging from the second level also serves as pieces of art. The buffet visually divides the dining room from the kitchen and offers plenty of space for food and drink.

*Above:* Sharing space with the kitchen and family room, this dining table is host to everything from homework to holiday gatherings. With leaves that can be reconfigured to fit any activity, the dining table adds the balance needed in the high-ceilinged, multi-functional room. An overhead light of twisted strands of wire serves as a piece of art as well as a functional light fixture.

*Left:* This custom dining table is highlighted by subtle overhead lighting. The glowing centerpiece resembles the fading sunset beyond, visible through the series of glass windows and sliding doors. Because the sky is ever-changing, this space is a favorite for breakfast at sunrise, dinner at sunset, or anytime in between.

*It is fun and whimsical to use a unique element in a formal space.*
*When entertaining, use an everyday item in an unexpected way. For*
*example, you can use a decorative birdbath on the dining room table*
*as a serving piece for bread or in the powder room as a towel holder.*
—CHAR DAVIS, *Owner, TC&T Construction*

*Opposite left:* The series of conical lighting above the contemporary dining table functions like a raised centerpiece. Paired with the flowers draped across the vase below, the effect is dramatic. Overhead glass cabinets hold stemware and the cabinets below house china and linens.

*Opposite right:* A grouping of nature's bounty awash in red—twigs, rocks, and plants—is under the glow of clustered light bulbs. These simple items give a unique twist to the dining space that could easily get lost in the corner. Separate yet easily accessible to the kitchen and family spaces, the dining area is an ideal area for kids to finish up homework while parents prepare dinner. *Right:* Amidst the predominantly black and brown coloring of this dining and living room space, the yellow bowl with orange and red Gerbera daisies brings color and energy to the home. A trio of light fixtures defines the dining space. The sitting area beyond is a logical place to have dessert and coffee, or begin the evening with cocktails.

The contrasting colors of the square-patterned floor mimic the design of the wooden ceiling beams. Slender arched windows marry the upper and lower spaces and frame outside views, and the use of tall trees and decorative curtains balance the room's colors and patterns. When not in use, your dining table is a perfect spot to display your favorite candles, jars, or objets d'art.

*The need for, or use of, any elevated lighting or acoustics in the home entertaining spaces are of no greater importance than other areas. A good architect or designer should take a holistic approach to the design, not placing a hierarchy in any one room.*
—MICHAEL P. JOHNSON, *Architect, Michael P. Johnson Design*

Engaging apricot-colored walls are a warm and colorful background for the signature painting and decorative wall sconces. The color also works beautifully with the darker furnishings. Strands of lighting hanging from the ceiling are functional and artistic. An oversized bottle shines in a niche.

A semi-circle of decorative iron sits atop a stone beam announcing the dining space inside. Potted greenery on either side of the opening frame the view. Under an iron chandelier, a round dining table and leather dining chairs are placed on a custom rug. Diners are treated to a charming view of the garden through a series of doors.

*Above: Saltillo tiles, natural wood beams, and green foliage in this dining room evoke an immediate sense of nature. Subtle wall colors allow the substantial pieces of furniture to take center stage and further accentuate the standing iron candelabra, iron chandelier, and the dark trim of the French doors. The dining room chairs are upholstered in colors that complement the flooring. Opposite: Throw open the doors and let the sunshine in! Take advantage of your doors and windows and use the natural light as part of your dining experience. The muted sounds of singing birds and gurgling fountains can be more satisfying than music. The casual nature of this dining room's wood paneling and dining table is blended with the more formal chandelier, dining chairs, and oil painting.*

Large pieces of original art are the focal points for this roomy dining room. Subtle spotlights on the ceiling highlight the paintings, while a series of windows above provides natural light. Painted in trompe l'oeil, the walls and arched entry resemble a castle and create an intimate feeling within the large space. An heirloom light fixture centers the classic table and surrounding leather dining chairs. The delicate mixture of trompe l'oeil and contemporary art is delightful.

A single piece of art tops the glowing fireplace and serves as an anchor for this dining area. Don't be afraid to move your dining table closer to favorite pieces of art, a fireplace, or an open window for special occasions. Sometimes a change in venue can motivate you to seek out even more creative ways to dine and entertain.

Be creative! Use mix-and-match chairs and your favorite china to create an eclectic dining experience. Pull a theme from a piece of art and let that be your guide. In this dining nook, a classic glass bowl mounded with lemons becomes a sensory centerpiece and ties in with the splashes of vibrant color from the painting.

*Top: A Native American painting sets the theme of this dining room. A rustic buffet table, iron wall sconces, and an elegant chandelier serve as strong décor elements softened by the white walls and honey-colored ceiling beams, door frames, and dining set. A rug holds a collection of painted wooden balls and two hefty metal candle sticks. Bottom: The muted shades of the wall art are used throughout the dining space and furnishings. Simple and elegant, the effect is peaceful and soothing. A wooden box holds a line of dried grasses as the perfect Southwest centerpiece.*

Anchored by an elevated fireplace, this dining room is energetic and inviting. Surrounding the fireplace are unusual shaped tiles that resemble the pattern on the chair fabric. The swirling designs of the bar cabinetry and wine storage doors are joined by the carved shapes on the chair backs. Outside, past the porch railing, mountain and city views are visible.

By using expansive glass panels and doors, this extended square dining table offers views from all seats. With a negative edge pool and golf course just outside and the mountains and cityscape beyond, the exterior environment becomes an integral part of the interior space.

*Opposite:* Who wouldn't be inspired with views like these! Four large, scenic windows offer diners seasonal enjoyment. Comfy chairs promise hours of relaxation for dining, working, having tea, or playing board games. A cantaloupe color was used on the wall above the windows and a soft sage below. The ceiling is a pale peach. All are perfect colors to blend subtly with the exterior surroundings.

*Above:* A casual dining spot is located near a cozy fireplace and a window offering a close-up look at the beauty of nature. Even on dreary days, this is an ideal spot to have glass of wine or read a book.

*Right: Hidden behind custom cabinetry, an entertainment center can enhance a family room's décor while maintaining its functional purpose.*

*Bottom left: Central to adjacent rooms, this is a favorite gathering spot for reading, relaxing, or listening to music. A television is discretely located behind the bookcase doors, and even in the loft above, family members can enjoy the sound system.*

*Left: What's behind those secret doors? The southwestern details are carried throughout the design and the entertainment center becomes a significant decorative element. A potted cactus, rustic throw pillows, and Native American crafts provide splashes of culture.*

The contemporary design of this family room purposely gives no hint of any high-tech presence. The media system, located behind cabinet doors, is easily accessed.

The typical living room is frequently the most expensive and the least used. But in this day and age, it makes little sense to have a beautiful room that is never used. Expand the use of the living room with a hidden television or a game table, or by using a door that leads to an outside patio to provide traffic flow for parties and other get-togethers.
—TONY SUTTON
Allied ASID, President &
Head Designer, Est Est, Inc.

This space has all the makings for a great family room. With the beehive fireplace, hidden entertainment center, bar/dining area, and comfortable seating, it effortlessly serves a variety of functions. And by using the same materials inside and outside—the flagstone flooring, stone accents, and wooden beams—the visual flow from the room to the patio is seamless.

*Top: Chairs you can sink in to and a roaring fire—what an ideal place to spend a quiet evening with family or to entertain friends. If needed, the TV and stereo system, concealed within the wooden doors, are at your fingertips. Close the drapery and you'll have a dark room to watch the latest blockbusters. Bottom: Although potentially bulky, the main benefit of an entertainment center is that it can accommodate the multiple components needed for today's high-tech systems. Whether custom made or not, armoires make ideal hosts for your growing entertainment system.*

*The most cost effective and efficient way to entertain is from one large gathering room, which is typically adjacent to, or part of, a large open kitchen area and family room that logically flows into a covered outdoor living area. The gathering area can be appointed with a full bar, fireplace, audio–video component, and plenty of room to stand, sit, and socialize. Ideally, the connected outdoor living area would be situated to capture some view, whether it be city lights or a view created through thoughtful landscape and hardscape architecture.*

—ANTHONY J. SALCITO, JR.

*Vice President, Salcito Custom Homes, Ltd.*

*Above:* The large screen projector system installed on the ceiling complements the clean lines of this media room. The wrap-around couch is comfortable for movie viewers and for other gatherings. The use of circles and squares throughout the room creates a pleasing symmetry.

*Right:* The open floor plan of this family/media space is delineated by the partition that holds a large screen television and a corner see-through fireplace. The benefit of a partial room divider is that outside views are not blocked from other areas of the home.

*The fabric-covered walls of this home theater offer additional sound absorption for those high drama flicks. The wall fabric pattern and colors coordinate with the special theater chairs and carpet that seem to transport you from the outside world into the movie of the moment. Against the wood-paneled backdrop, three screens allow everyone to see from all angles. And because theaters are traditionally cold, snuggly throw blankets are waiting on each chair.*

*Opposite: A western-themed movie theater in your own home! Individual movie theater seats with cup holders await your arrival. Old western movie posters and accessories like the framed leather chaps, lariat, and gun complement the faux-finished walls, wood accents, and velvet fringed curtains. It's show time! Top: A symphony in blue, the seating in this home theater conjures up images of midnight movies. Cushy pillows and blankets adorn the chairs and lavender theater curtains are ready to part when the movie begins. Don't forget the popcorn! An old-fashioned popcorn popper is placed close by. Bottom: The red and blue color scheme of this entertainment room is as impressive as any grand theater. Red chairs and a blue ceiling pick up the colors from the shimmering curtains. Touches of brown ground the energy. With seats placed on two levels, everyone has unobstructed views of the screen.*

*Above:* For easy access, creatively use the space under center islands or wall cabinets to store everything you need for your next party. Although storing your wine in a temperature-controlled environment is optimum, storing wine bottles on their sides is strongly recommended for all wine. *Right:* Space under stairs is oftentimes wasted, but it can be the perfect nook to hold wine. Here, a built-in beverage bar rests in a recessed arch next to the wine center, creating a dedicated area for entertaining.

Top left: Using wine storage as part of a room's décor is made easier with glass doors. An unused closet or cabinet can be redesigned to hold your special bottles.

Above: Like a pantry, wine storage can be an integral part of the kitchen. With a French door and decorative iron, it becomes a focal point for the room. Bottom left: All you need is a table, some chairs, and a little space to create your own private wine space. Using stone and wood, this wine room is similar in feel to those found in wineries.

With room for a favorite sculpture, the cellar walls are entirely for storage. A charming table for two offers a place to sit, sip, and relax.

*Above:* With his eye on the bottles, the sommelier pig holds center stage in this cellar. Storage rises to the ceiling and is easily accessed with the ladder. *Left:* Taking advantage of unused space, this wine cellar is unusual in its shape but extremely efficient and well organized. Extra storage for collectible wooden wine cases is above with shelving and cabinets for glassware and other wine necessities fitting perfectly.

For those dedicated to the collection and consumption of fine wine, temperature-controlled wine cellars are the ultimate special space. With a grape-designed iron entry door, this room has a separate seating area decorated with wine-themed accessories and a perfect view of the storage area beyond.

# Rejuvenate

*Right:* The ability to experience nature—ideally from outside or from generous views inside—is an important part of relaxing your mind, body, and soul. Here, there are plenty of opportunities to do that both inside and out. Comfortable seating on the patio brings the environment to your feet. Sip a glass of wine, feel the fresh air, and reconnect with yourself or a loved one. Inside, surrounding windows allow complete views and a chance to star gaze, dream, and ponder the wonder of life. *Opposite:* Sun porches are about comfort, relaxation, and the pleasure of the outdoors while retaining the ease of indoor living. Wicker chairs, plump cushions, favorite magazines, and a cup of tea hold the promise of a leisurely afternoon.

# { Body and Soul }

ONE OF THE MOST IMPORTANT QUALITIES about your home is that you feel comfortable living there. Because no matter what kind of design or style surrounds you, your house won't feel like home unless it appeals to you in ways that matter to your soul.

Many people find joy and enlightenment in certain types of rooms. Deciding what gives you pleasure is the first step in creating that space. For example, readers, historians, and intellectuals might be drawn to the idea of having a library dedicated to books, maps, and important documents, and adorned with comfy seating, a good reading lamp, and if possible, a fireplace.

Others find inspiration in art studios and hobby rooms. With a space that is your own, it is easy to slip inside, close the door, and become lost in your creativity. With this kind of room, designing it to your heart's content is pure bliss.

Sunrooms have long been a favorite space for relaxing alone or with the family, particularly in the Southwest. Flooded with light and views of the outdoors, these cozy rooms offer a hint of being outside while enjoying protection from the elements. Sipping afternoon tea or a glass of wine before dinner seems more enjoyable when doing so from the sunroom's white wicker rocker or overstuffed down couch.

Other areas of the home can be dedicated to the body. The act of exercise releases positive energy into the body and helps to maintain your health. Exercise rooms, popular in today's home, help you stay focused by having the space available and the equipment necessary to get a good workout.

On a calmer level is meditation and quiet time. Increasingly, more homes are designed to include an area or separate space specifically for meditation, yoga, or other reflective practice. Especially in today's multi-faceted lives, this space might be exactly what is needed to maintain your balance. The overall goal is to discover what makes you dream, create, or relax, and then design a space that allows it to happen.

*Top:* Carve out a special space to be with your favorite books. You'll need a chair to sink in to, a footrest, adequate lighting, and ideally, a fireplace. The rich colors of stone and wood in this charming library add to the southwestern theme. Natural light from the series of windows gives a warm glow to the room during the day.

*Bottom:* Looking for something to do with a small nook or alcove? Create floor to ceiling bookshelves, one of the most efficient uses of space for tight areas. If there is room, add a desk for writing or a chair for reading.

Clearing, cleansing, composing. These three steps are necessary to create a relaxing and rejuvenating space. Removing the clutter is essential. Cleansing every surface livens the air. And, composing your space with simple essentials offers the feeling of order. The goal is for each object to contribute aesthetically in texture, color, line, and proportion, yet be restful to contemplate. Natural materials—wood, stone, plants, bamboo, and water—are the most soothing. Tibetan bells to ring, a small fountain with running water, or musical recordings that take you away are other peaceful elements to consider.

—JEANNIE BEAL MARINI
*Designer & Author, Your Design Zone*

Grab a book and settle in for a long, satisfying read. Bookshelves can fit in almost any space in the home, and no space is more pleasant than an area dedicated to comfort with cushy furniture, an enchanting fireplace, and access to the outdoors.

As more people become chemically sensitive, we need to look at options that protect our health and our environment. Some of these products include non-toxic wood flooring, wool carpet, cork flooring, linoleum, fabrics, furniture, tile, cabinets, and stains. Besides being earth- and people-friendly, these options are high quality and visually beautiful. Removing items from your home that are oil based or made of particle board is a good start. Contact your local Green Building Program (www.gbpc.org) for a list of professionals who specialize in environmental planning and design.

—SARAH GREENE
Designer, The Greene Room

*Opposite:* **A captivating painting might be the inspiration for your designated meditation space. This realistic Native American scene is powerful in its color and symbolism, encouraging viewers to take some time to stop and ponder its message.** *Left:* **Do you long to retreat to a calm, quiet place? The restful hues of this inviting space are conducive to spending some quiet time alone or with loved ones. The vibrant painting over the fireplace is the focal point of this warm, cozy den.** *Above:* **What gives you joy and lifts your heart? Perhaps it is a particular piece of art or a cherished collection. Use those elements in your home and establish areas that make you smile. In this room, an energetic painting and natural sunlight create a happy, healthy environment.**

To follow the philosophy of feng shui in your home, the principals of orientation, harmony, and positive energy (chi) are needed. Common to the Southwest, for example, are rooms that are filled with bright, hot sunlight. To counteract this glare, add window treatments that screen the sun or change the color of the walls to a cool color of blue. This balance, according to feng shui, will help welcome good fortune into your life.

—GABRIELLE ROECKELEIN, *Allied ASID, President, Park Avenue Design*

*Above:* **Passionate about your view? Design an interior area that is committed to helping you take advantage of your outdoor spaces. With doors that open to the exterior of this home, an iron railing protects children and pets from escaping yet allows fresh air and fragrance to tickle the senses.** *Right:* **When creating a furniture layout for your rooms, don't underestimate the need for seating. Areas oftentimes overlooked are against walls or in corners where two chairs and a table or an overstuffed chaise can be both practical and an integral part of the overall furniture arrangement.**

A simple beehive fireplace has become the focal point for this seating nook. Large chairs upholstered in red stand out against the yellow and gold tones of the highly textured wall and catch the filtered sunlight through the sheer drapes. A whimsical design on the fireplace suggests the shapes of the flickering flames below. Using a collection of candles in the fireplace instead of a fire is a romantic alternative. The bunch of apples ensconced in the silver pedestal unites the scene.

*Top:* With contiguous views framed by butt-glazed windows, daily exercise regimes are elevated to inspiring. If planning to create a separate exercise space—either new or in an existing area—take advantage of the power of windows with views, or use your favorite art or special mementos as visual motivation.

*Bottom:* The sound of moving water does something to the spirit. Ponds, streams, and fountains—whether inside or out—are natural relaxants. Just off the patio, a set of wicker chairs nestled beside a flowing stream of water offers a place to sit and think, write, read, or enjoy the beautiful sunsets.

*Opposite:* Professionals recommend finding a special space solely dedicated to the relaxation of your mind, body, and soul. Candles glowing, this peaceful room is spacious enough to hold a massage table with room left over for daily yoga practice. The colors are tranquil and the accessories enhance rather than disrupt the flow of the room.

# Work & Play

*Right:* Can't do two things at once? Try four! This game room is a favorite place to be when trying to watch multiple channels at the same time. A room the whole family can enjoy, the game table is host to card and board games, homework, and an occasional meal. *Opposite:* Discover your passions and then make room for them in your home. Whether it is playing cards or putting your feet up at the end of the day, multi-functional rooms can accommodate everyone's desires. When you're not outside playing golf, slip inside to try your hand at cards, or take a nap on an overstuffed couch.

# { *creating a balanced home* }

THEY SAY LIFE IS A BALANCING ACT—work, kids, significant other, pets, yourself. Your home, ideally a haven for you and your family, is the center of your balancing act. From there you are able to organize, plan, play, work, and rest. Making sure you have the tools and space to do that is crucial when it comes to your home environment.

Kids are energetic, creative, and individual. They are little people with big needs, including lots of space. Making sure they have the room to grow, play, and learn is important when looking at designing their spaces. Playrooms, games areas, study nooks, reading corners, and art space—all can foster a sense of self and discovery. And don't forget your need for play as well. Carve out space for your favorite activity whether it is billiards, chess, piano, or even photography.

Likewise, identifying a space for your work is equally essential. Home offices or dedicated workspaces make the process of working and organizing your life at home more efficient. Add window exposure to soak up the southwestern sun, wall space for a favorite piece of art, and a chair conducive to conjuring up your best ideas, and you'll never want to leave this special space.

Finally, but not the least significant, is the space you provide for your beloved animal friends. Handmade doggie beds, raised cat runs, antique bird cages, and incredible fish tanks only hint at the special place these precious beings have in your heart.

There is nothing more vital to your sense of home than the ability to handle the myriad of responsibilities and personalities that make up your life. Working towards that sense of peace and balance is motivating, exciting, exhausting, and oh so very rewarding.

When your home office shares space with another room in the house, space and design considerations become even more important. For example, if your work space is in the family room, you may need to establish a work station that can be converted back to a general family area when needed by using built-in cabinets, pull-out drawers, and a table-top desk that can be closed when no longer in use.

—LISA DELL'OSSO, *Partner & Designer, Cathedral Interiors*

*Above:* This is an office space made for work and relaxation. The custom desk is neat and efficient and clutter is kept to a minimum with built-in cabinetry and storage closets. A fireplace in the corner and a comfortable chair and ottoman encourage daily breaks to replenish energy and provide inspiration. *Top right:* With an entrance from the house and a separate entrance from the exterior, this is the ideal home office for those who need to meet with clients without interfering with the rest of the household, or vice versa. The custom wood desk is made of the same wood as the doors and ceiling beams. *Bottom right:* The beauty of this home office is made more visible to the rest of the home with sliding glass-paneled doors. The see-through doors also serve to allow privacy when needed, yet they also eliminate the closed-in feeling that small spaces can sometimes create. *Opposite:* If there isn't enough room to have a separate office space, consider using a room divider. The decorative glass panels on the top of this divider allow light into the small office while the solid wood design below assures privacy. The Mission-style home office is efficient and organized, and it even has space to display a cherished pottery collection.

This game room boasts plenty of activities—from the bar and game table to the billiard table to the seating for the big screen. Understanding how you like to spend your free time and entertain others will help you plan your ideal space, and it will help you decide whether or not it needs to be a separate room or shared with another space.

It is amazing what can fit into a small space when it is organized. If you need storage for CDs, toys, art, or electronics, look no further than your blank wall. In addition to shelves, niches and other sculptural wall elements can add both function and design to your interior spaces.

—HOWARD SPARER
*Owner & Designer, Wall Sculptures*

One of the biggest challenges encountered when designing a game room is making sure there is enough space for all the "toys." For example, a pool table should have at least five feet around it for people to play safely. And many times, wet bars and theater rooms are attached so plan-ning for traffic flow and viewing opportunities from all of these locations are important considerations.

—DEBRA MAY HIMES, *ASID,*
*IIDA, Debra May Himes Interior Design*

*Above:* A dedicated billiards room has plenty of seating and good lighting. Pool tables can be made to complement any design style, and some even come with tops that con-vert into a board room-style table. *Left:* The log pole-style of this pool table is in perfect harmony with the Southwest-themed recreation room. When planning to add a pool table to your home, make sure you measure the space needed to include adequate room for using the pool cues.

*Top:* Accents of blue—from the patterned rug to the overhead light—create an electric energy in this game room. The chocolate-colored walls are complemented by the use of stone on the floor and natural rock around the fire feature. And there is enough space surrounding the pool table to comfortably accommodate any and all players. *Bottom:* Reminiscent of times gone by, this ornate bar would be an eye-catcher at any modern-day saloon. With the decorative wood carving and hand-painted design on the panels, the bar is a fine fit with the artwork displayed in the room. *Opposite:* Bright colors, easy-to-maintain furniture, and a plethora of fun things to do—this recreation room will interest children and adults for hours. With chess sets at the ready, the mood of this room is comfortable, eclectic, and engaging. Oversized prints and retro signage give added spark to the red walls. The fireplace and a grouping of candles lend a touch of sophistication to this dynamic space.

# { *acknowledgements* }

WORKING ON THIS BOOK has been a growth process for me in terms of rediscovering what I need and want in my interior spaces in order to make them feel as peaceful and comfortable as possible. As with any life change, the addition of small children in my life has refocused some of my priorities! ☼ Fortunately, it is easy to make changes in our homes that reflect where we are and where we want to be. Taking the advice of professionals and examining the results of their work captured in the photos of this book has been instrumental in helping me create spaces that make my home life meaningful. I hope you will be motivated as well. ☼ Not all writers are fortunate enough to have an incredible editor. Tammy Gales-Biber, who was also my guide on my first book—*Outdoor Style: The Essence of Southwest Living*—makes my job easy and delightful. And David Jenney has created another outstanding book with his eye for design and detail. It was my good luck to have landed in their hands—twice! ☼ Many of these outstanding homes were found by the multi-talented team at *Phoenix Home & Garden*. I am indebted to editor Linda J. Barkman and art director/photo stylist Margie Van Zee for their discoveries. The images they procured for *Phoenix Home & Garden* have fortuitously found themselves inside these pages. ☼ As demonstrated throughout the book, some of the most gifted photographers have contributed their work to this project. And for this I am grateful. Photographing home interiors is complicated and these professionals make it look effortless. They continue to amaze me with their artistic ability and delightful images. ☼ The professionals who shared their words of wisdom and guidance on the pages throughout this book are talented, creative, and passionately dedicated to their profession. I am thankful that they were willing to share some of their insights and ideas on how to design space that is functional, beautiful, and personal. ☼ And, as always, where would I be without my friends and family—my support system? Heartfelt thanks go to Eileen, Paulina, Shelly, Martie, Shannon, Stacey, Julia, Nancy, Margaret, Monica, Pamela, Gloria, Julie, Dyan, Kim, Doug, Michele, Naomi, Frances, Lisa, Catherine, Sara, Pam, Gabrielle, Marla, and The Book Club. ☼ My husband John is a daily inspiration. He is one of the most creative and caring persons I know, and I can't imagine my life without him. His unwavering support is a gift from and to the heart. Our son Neo and daughter Eco are shining stars. To me, they represent all that life is supposed to be.

Linda J. Barkman
Editor
*Phoenix Home & Garden*
Scottsdale, AZ
480/664-3960
www.phgmag.com

Paula Berg
Interior Designer
Paula Berg Design Associates
Scottsdale, AZ
480/998-2344
Park City, UT
435/655-9443
pbergdesign@aol.com

Denny Collins
Photographer
Denny Collins Photo
Phoenix, AZ
602/381-0828
www.DennyCollins.com

Charles Cunniffe
Architect
Charles Cunniffe Architects
Aspen, CO
970/925-5590
www.Cunniffe.com

Char Davis
Owner
TC&T Construction
Phoenix, AZ
480/296-9454

Lisa Dell'Osso
Partner & Designer
Cathedral Interiors
San Francisco, CA
415/665-8895
Paradise Valley, AZ
480/367-0956

Kevin Duermit
Vice President
Toll Brothers, Inc.
Scottsdale, AZ
480/951-0782
www.tollbrothersinc.com

Sharon Alber Fannin, ASID
Designer & Owner
Jody Ramsay, Allied ASID
Designer
Fannin Interiors
Phoenix, AZ
602/840-8088
www.FanninInteriors.com

Tom Fisher
President & CEO
Fisher Custom Homes, LLC
Scottsdale, AZ
480/585-7350
800/587-7350
www.FisherCustomHomes.com

Marcia Graber
Designer
Graber Designs, Ltd.
Scottsdale, AZ
480/998-0989
graberdesigns@cox.net

Jeffrey Green
Photographer
Jeffrey Green Photography
Las Vegas, NV & Phoenix, AZ
702/257-1655
www.jgreenphoto.com

Sarah Greene
Designer
The Greene Room
Scottsdale, AZ
602/622-6481
TheGreeneRoom@aol.com

Kim E. Gwozdz
Designer & Owner
Provenance
Phoenix, AZ
602/912-8552
602/332-8332

Deneice Hase
Design Director
Robb & Stucky
Scottsdale, AZ
480/922-0011
www.RobbStucky.com

Tony Hernandez
Photographer
Hernandez Photography
Phoenix, AZ
602/870-8070
thphoto@qwest.net

Jamie Herzlinger, Allied ASID
Designer & Owner
Jamie Herzlinger Interiors
Scottsdale, AZ
602/795-3824
JamieHerz@aol.com

Michael Higgins
Architect & Owner
Higgins Architects, LLC
Scottsdale, AZ
480/990-8897
www.higginsarch.com

Debra May Himes, ASID, IIDA
Designer & Owner
Debra May Himes Interior Design &
Associates, LLC
Chandler, AZ
480/497-2699
debra.himes@dmhdesign.com

Michael P. Johnson
Architect
Michael P. Johnson Design Studios,
Ltd.
Cave Creek, AZ
480/488-2691
www.mpjstudio.com

Bess J. Jones, Allied ASID
Designer & Owner
Bess Jones Interiors
Scottsdale, AZ
480/443-8770
bessjonesinteriors@earthlink.net

Nancy Kitchell
Designer
Kitchell Interior Design Associates
Scottsdale, AZ
480/951-0280
kidaaz@aol.com

Marilyn Joy-Kolesar
Designer
MJK Designs, LLC
Paradise Valley, AZ
480/596-0055
mjkdesign@cox.net

Jana Parker Lee, Allied ASID
Partner & Senior Designer
Wiseman & Gale Interiors
Scottsdale, AZ
480/945-8447
www.wisemanandgale.com

Eric Linthicum
President
Linthicum Custom Builders
Scottsdale, AZ
480/515-1700
www.linthicumconstructors.com

Jeannie Beal Marini
Designer & Author
Your Design Zone
Scottsdale, AZ
480/222-0237
jeanniebealmarini@yahoo.com

Julia Redwine, ASID
Interior Designer
Studio One Design
Wheeling, IL
847/229-7000

Brad Reed
Photographer
Brad Reed Photography
Phoenix, AZ
602/317-9800
www.bradreedphotography.com

Gabrielle Roeckelein, Allied ASID
President
Park Avenue Design, Inc.
Chandler, AZ
480/961-7779
www.ParkAvenueDesign.com

Catherine Ross
Certified Professional Coach
Start Now Coaching
Phoenix, AZ
480/990-1068
www.startnowcoach.com

Anthony J. Salcito, Jr.
Vice President
Salcito Custom Homes, Ltd.
Scottsdale, AZ
480/585-5065
www.Salcito.com

Charles Schiffner
Principal & President
Charles Schiffner & Associates
Phoenix, AZ
602/954-7442
crschiffner@juno.com

Linda Seeger
Interior Designer
Seeger Interior Design
Scottsdale, AZ
480/348-2776
Linda@SeegerInteriorDesign.com

Marieann Green Seeger,
ASID, IIDA
President & Principal Designer
Marieann Green Interior Design, Inc.
Scottsdale, AZ
480/473-1122

Pam Singleton
Photographer
Image Photography
Scottsdale, AZ
480/946-3246
www.photoexcursions.com

Christy Smith
President
Casas del Oso Luxury Homes
Scottsdale, AZ
480/502-8408
www.casasdeloso.com

Suzanne Smith, Allied ASID
Suzanne Smith Interior Designs, Ltd.
Paradise Valley, AZ
480/368-0370
suzasid@cox.net

Howard Sparer
Owner & Designer
Wall Sculptures, Inc.
Phoenix, AZ
602/493-1870
www.wallsculptures.com

Tony Sutton, Allied ASID
President & Head Designer
Est Est, Inc.
Scottsdale, AZ
480/563-1555
www.estestinc.com

Dino Tonn
Photographer
Dino Tonn Photography
Scottsdale, AZ
602/765-0455
www.dinotonn.com

John Trotto
Photographer
John Trotto Photography, Inc.
Phoenix, AZ
480/759-6500
www.johntrotto.com

Sarah Swartz Wessel
Architect
Tennen Studio
Phoenix, AZ
602/840-8625
www.tennenstudio.com

Linda Whiteaker
Interior Designer
Whiteaker Design
Scottsdale, AZ
480/473-1341

D. Kristine Woolsey
Architect
Woolsey Studio, Inc.
Tempe, AZ
480/945-3440
www.woolseystudio.com

David Zilly
Photographer
David Zilly Photography
Phoenix, AZ
602/262-2880
www.davidzillyphotos.com

Scot Zimmerman
Photographer
Scot Zimmerman Photography
Heber City, UT
800/279-2757
scotzman@sprynet.com

Jeff Zischke
Artist & Designer
Zischke Studio
Scottsdale, AZ
480/483-9225
www.zischkestudio.com

# { *photo credits* }

Photography © 2005 by:

Jeff Green: front cover, ii–iii, 7 (top right), 9, 15 (top left), 18, 19 (top left), 20 (bottom), 26 (bottom left), 28, 32 (top left), 39 (bottom), 40, 41, 42 (top left and bottom), 44, 45 (top left), 46 (bottom), 52, 53 (bottom), 54 (bottom), 58 (bottom), 59, 60, 61 (top), 65 (bottom), 71, 73, 78 (top left and bottom left), 83 (top), 90, 95, 97, 103 (right), 104 (bottom left and bottom right), 107 (bottom), 112 (right), 121 (right), 122 (left), 123, 129, back cover

Brad Reed: back flap (author photo)

Pam Singleton: 7 (bottom right), 16 (top), 36, 42 (right), 61 (bottom), 77 (left and top right), 85, 86, 91 (bottom), 99 (left), 100 (bottom), 103 (left), 110, 119, 120, 122 (right)

Dino Tonn, Architecture by RJ Bacon Co., Cabinets by European Design: 37 (top), 109

Dino Tonn, Interior design by Sherrie Conquest Interiors: 116 (right)

Dino Tonn, Interior design by Sandy Cozens Design: 69

Dino Tonn, Interior design by Teresa DeLellis, Architecture by RJ Bacon Co., Built by DeLellis Development: 128 (bottom)

Dino Tonn, Interior design by Do Daz: 132 (top)

Dino Tonn, Interior design by Est Est, Inc., Built by Kitchell Custom Homes: 111 (bottom)

Dino Tonn, Interior design by Fannin Interiors: 64 (top left)

Dino Tonn, Interior design by Graber Designs: 38 (bottom), 50, 51, 76 (right), 82, 83 (bottom)

Dino Tonn, Interior design by Marieann Green Seeger: 6, 20 (top right), 45 (bottom left), 55, 84 (right), 106, 107 (top), 127

Dino Tonn, Interior design by Jamie Herzlinger Interiors: 12, 13, 29, 32 (right), 33, 34, 63, 81 (top right), 88, 98

Dino Tonn, Interior design by Donna Jantz Design: 67 (bottom)

Dino Tonn, Interior design by Bess Jones: vi, 2 (right), 24, 25, 48 (right), 56, 57, 79 (left), 81 (left and bottom right), 96 (left), 101, 128 (top left)

Dino Tonn, Interior design by Deborah May Himes: 8, 17, 54 (top), 70 (right), 80, 94, 134

Dino Tonn, Interior design by Carol Minchew Interiors: 96 (right)

Dino Tonn: Built by Nance Construction: 132 (bottom)

Dino Tonn, Interior design by Ashley P. Designs: 111 (top)

Dino Tonn, Interior design by Pembrook Lane Interiors: 66

Dino Tonn, Built by RS Homes: vi, 24, 25 (top), 57, 81 (left), 128 (top left)

Dino Tonn, Interior design by Shellie Rudow Interiors: 68

Dino Tonn, Built by Salcito Custom Homes: 56, 96 (left)

Dino Tonn, Interior design by Kim Shaw Interiors: 89

Dino Tonn, Built by Shiloh Custom Homes: 25 (bottom), 79 (left), 101, 111 (top)

Dino Tonn, Architecture by Urban Design Associates: vi, 2, 24, 25, 48 (right), 57, 79 (left), 81, 101, 128 (top left)

Dino Tonn, Interior design by Wiseman & Gale: 19 (top right), 30 (top right), 49, 75 (bottom), 112 (top left)

John Trotto: 15 (bottom left), 38 (top), 74, 114 (bottom left and right), 117

David Zilly: 14 (top), 35 (top), 47, 115

Scot Zimmerman: 3, 7 (top left), 10 (top left), 14 (bottom), 16 (bottom), 19 (bottom), 20 (top left), 21, 23 (middle left and bottom left), 31, 35 (bottom), 43, 45 (right), 48 (top left), 62, 64 (right), 67 (top left and top right), 70 (top left), 72, 77 (bottom right), 78 (right), 79 (top right), 84 (top left and bottom left), 91 (top), 92, 93, 102, 108 (top), 113 (bottom left and right), 118, 121 (left), 131, 133

Courtesy of Denny Collins: 99 (right)

Courtesy of Est Est, Inc., Photography by Tony Hernandez: 15 (right), 27, 30 (top left and bottom), 58 (top), 75 (top), 87, 114 (top left), 116 (top left), 124 (top), 126 (top left), 128 (top right), 130

Courtesy of Fannin Interiors, Photography by Mark Boisclair: 26 (right)

Courtesy of Fannin Interiors, Photography by Lydia Cutter: 23 (top left), 105

Courtesy of Fannin Interiors, Photography by R. Henderson: 26 (top left)

Courtesy of Marieann Green Seeger, Interior Design, Photography by Erhard Pfeiffer: 53 (top), 113 (top left)

Courtesy of Marieann Green Seeger, Interior Design, Photography by Walt Saadus: 46 (top), 76 (top left), 100 (top)

Courtesy of Kim Gwozdz, Designer, Photography by Mark Boisclair: 22 (top)

Courtesy of Michael P. Johnson Design Studios. Ltd., Photography by Bill Timmerman: 10 (bottom left and right), 11, 22 (bottom), 23 (right), 37 (bottom), 65 (top), 108 (bottom)

Courtesy of Toll Brothers, Homebuilders, Photography by Mark Boisclair: front flap, 2 (top left), 5, 104 (top), 126 (right)

Courtesy of Toll Brothers, Homebuilders, Photography by Greg Cava: 4 (bottom), 124 (bottom), 125

Courtesy of Toll Brothers, Homebuilders, Photography by Rob Muir: 39 (top)

Courtesy of Toll Brothers, Homebuilders, Photography by Scott Sandler: 4 (top)